HOW Movies ARE MADE

by Noah Leatherland

Minneapolis, Minnesota

Credits

Images are courtesy of Shutterstock.com, unless otherwise stated. COVER & RECURRING – photka, Aggapom Poomitu, Quarta, Macrovector, Bagel Studio, Chief Design, Dooder, Rolau Elena, Natasha Pankina, Alena Nv. 4–5 – VH-studio, Zoriana Zaitseva. 6–7 – Studio Romantic, Yuganov Konstantin. 8–9 – hxdbzxy, New Africa. 10–11 – Pixel-Shot, New Africa, guruXOX. 12–13– Gorodenkoff, Nejron Photo. 14–15 – Filip Fuxa, Stefano Tammaro. 16–17 – Lia Koltyrina, Gorodenkoff. 18–19 – khamidi setyobudi, Jos Temprano, Alex from the Rock. 20–21 – Gorodenkoff, Frame Stock Footage. 22–23 – Deliris, PrinceOfLove. 24–25 – Gorodenkoff, Frame Stock Footage. 26–27 – Stefan.Simonovski, New Africa. 28–29 – KOTOIMAGES, Ground Picture. 30–31 – ViDI Studio.

Bearport Publishing Company Product Development Team

Publisher: Jen Jenson; Director of Product Development: Spencer Brinker; Editorial Director: Allison Juda; Editor: Cole Nelson; Editor: Tiana Tran; Production Editor: Naomi Reich; Art Director: Kim Jones; Designer: Kayla Eggert; Designer: Steve Scheluchin; Production Specialist: Owen Hamlin

Library of Congress Cataloging-in-Publication Data is available at www.loc.gov or upon request from the publisher.

ISBN: 979-8-89577-085-6 (hardcover)
ISBN: 979-8-89577-475-5 (paperback)
ISBN: 979-8-89577-202-7 (ebook)

© 2026 BookLife Publishing
This edition is published by arrangement with BookLife Publishing.

North American adaptations © 2026 Bearport Publishing Company. All rights reserved. No part of this publication may be reproduced in whole or in part, stored in any retrieval system, or transmitted in any form or by any means, electronic, mechanical, photocopying, recording, or otherwise, without written permission from the publisher. Bearport Publishing is a division of FlutterBee Education Group.

For more information, write to Bearport Publishing, 3500 American Blvd W, Suite 150, Bloomington, MN 55431.

Contents

How Things Are Made 4
Ideas and Imagination 6
Script Writing .8
Casting. 10
Costumes, Hair, and Makeup. 12
Props and Sets 14
Filming. 16
Stunts. 18
Visual Effects 20
Sound and Music 22
Editing 24
Promotion 26
Release 28
Your Next Project. 30
Glossary 31
Index 32
Read More. 32
Learn More Online 32

How Things Are Made

Are you a creative person?

Your favorite books, movies, TV shows, and video games came from the minds of people just like you!

Movies are stories that play out on the screen. You can see them in movie theaters or at home from your own couch.

It takes a group of talented people to turn a concept into a blockbuster movie.

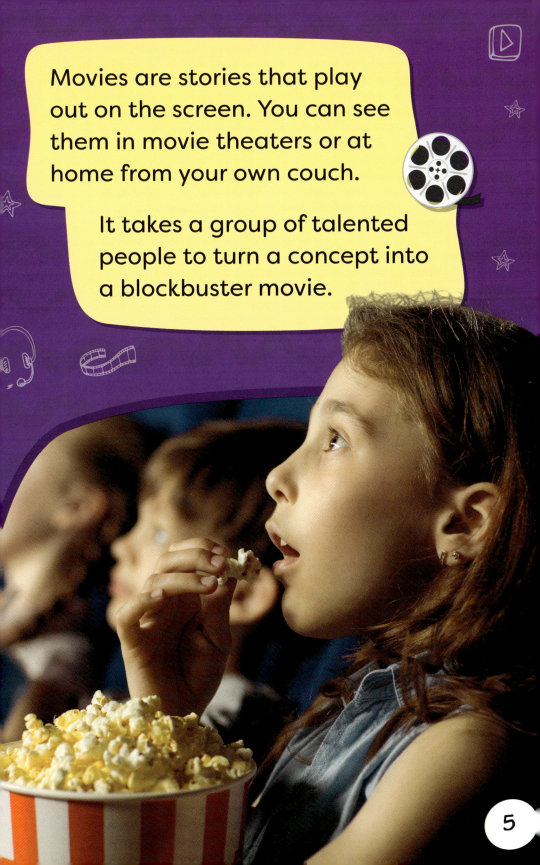

Ideas and Imagination

The first step in movie making is coming up with an idea.

A movie can be funny, scary, or dramatic. It can take place in the real world or somewhere magical.

Any idea can become a movie. You just need a good team and some imagination.

Script Writing

The next step is often to write a script. Movie writers, called screenwriters, form the story and come up with characters.

A script will often include information about the **setting**. This is where the movie takes place. The script is broken into different **scenes**.

Scripts contain descriptions of all the things that the movie's actors will do. They also have everything the actors will say. This is called dialogue.

Often, screenwriters rewrite a script many times until it is just right.

Casting

Next, it is time to find the actors to play the characters. This is called casting. The movie makers invite actors to audition for parts.

Each actor gives a short performance so the movie makers can see if they are right for a role.

The actors who are picked to be in the movie are called the cast.

They are given scripts so that they can learn their lines. They often practice as a group.

Actors need good memories to learn all their lines.

Costumes, Hair, and Makeup

The actors need to be fitted for clothing. Everything an actor wears is chosen by costume designers.

Sometimes, costumes look like everyday clothes. But other times, designers need to create historical clothes, spacesuits, or even superhero costumes!

Movies also have hair and makeup artists. These artists make sure the actors look right on camera.

Sometimes, these artists add **prosthetics**. Prosthetics are fake body parts.

Prosthetic heads

13

Props and Sets

Before a movie can be made, a prop master needs to gather the props.

These are the objects that are seen and used in movies. Some props are everyday objects. But others need to be made.

Sometimes, real-world locations are used for filming. Other times, sets have to be built.

Set **designers** work with builders to make castles, alien planets, haunted houses, and more.

Many movie sets only look real from the front.

Filming

With the costumes, props, and sets taken care of, filming can begin. Directors are in charge of everything on set.

Camera crews make sure that they film everything the directors want. Sound teams record everything the actors say.

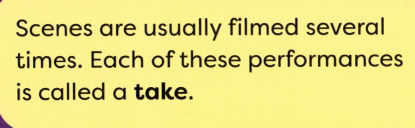

Scenes are usually filmed several times. Each of these performances is called a **take**.

For each take, the director might have the actors say their lines differently. Later, the director can decide which one is best.

A green screen

Some scenes are filmed on a green screen set. The background is added in later.

Stunts

Action scenes can be some of the most exciting parts of movies. They can also include dangerous **stunts**. These are often done by trained stunt teams instead of the actors.

Stunt performers know how to safely drive fast, crash through glass, and do other dangerous things.

Stunt performers use lots of special equipment so they don't get hurt. Wires let them jump through the air safely.

Stunt performers also learn how to land safely after falling from high places.

Visual Effects

Not everything you see in movies exists in real life. Many things are added to scenes after filming.

Visual effects artists use computers to place things into movies. They try to make them look as real as possible.

Visual effects can transform a few people into a large crowd. They can make actors look like strange creatures.

You might not notice everything that is added with visual effects. A lot of it is in the background.

Sound and Music

Sound designers add sounds to scenes after they are filmed. Creaky doors or speeding cars can make a scene more exciting.

These designers also create sounds that may not exist in real life, such as space lasers and monster roars.

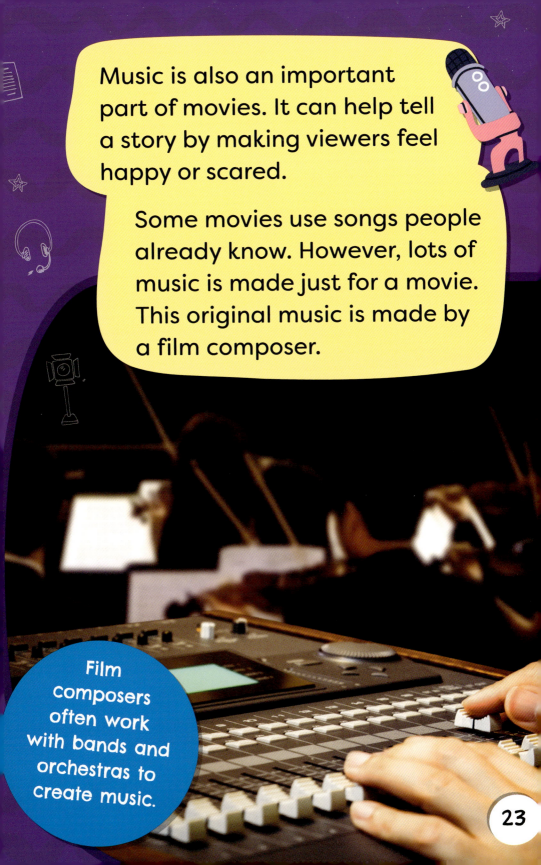

Music is also an important part of movies. It can help tell a story by making viewers feel happy or scared.

Some movies use songs people already know. However, lots of music is made just for a movie. This original music is made by a film composer.

Film composers often work with bands and orchestras to create music.

Editing

Once filming is done and all the parts of a movie are ready, they have to be put together.

The director works with **editors** to pick the best takes. Then, the editors put all the scenes, effects, and sounds together.

Not everything that has been filmed can fit into the movie. Some scenes might be cut out completely.

Editors have to think about every part of a movie very carefully to make sure it all works together.

Promotion

Movie studios promote their movies to get people excited about them.

Designers make posters to display in movie theaters and in public places. They work hard to make them eye-catching.

Editors put together clips from movies to make short videos called trailers. Trailers get posted online and shown in movie theaters.

A movie's cast and director might also do interviews. These help get more people interested in seeing the movie.

Release

The movie is finished! Now, it is time to show it to people.

A premiere is when a movie is shown for the first time. Some movie premieres happen at **film festivals**. Others are their own big events with lots of guests.

Many movies are shown in movie theaters. People buy tickets to see the movie on a big screen.

Other movies are available online. This makes it easy for people to watch movies without leaving their homes.

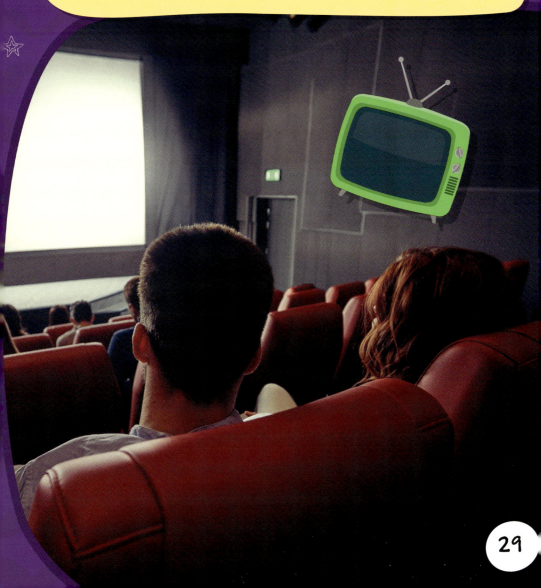

Your Next Project

Many creative people work together to make movies. It takes a lot of teamwork.

What job would you do to help make a movie? The next big blockbuster could be yours!

Glossary

designers people who plan and help create something

editors people who put video footage together

film festivals events where many movies are shown

promote to show something off

prosthetics fake body parts that are added to a person's body

setting the location in which a story takes place

stunts tricks and dangerous acts that take skill to perform safely

take a recording of an action or scene in a movie

visual effects computer-made details or images that are added to scenes after filming

Index

actors 9–13, 16–18, 21
auditions 10
cameras 13, 16
computers 20
designers 12, 15, 22, 26
directors 16–17, 24, 27
movie theaters 5, 26–27, 29
premieres 28
scripts 8–9, 11
trailers 27

Read More

Leatherland, Noah. *How Anime and Cartoons Are Made (From Concept to Creation).* Minneapolis: Bearport Publishing Company, 2026.

Shaw, Mary. *The Art of Film (Amazing Art Forms).* Minneapolis: Abdo Publishing, 2025.

Learn More Online

1. Go to **FactSurfer.com** or scan the QR code below.
2. Enter **"Movies"** into the search box.
3. Click on the cover of this book to see a list of websites.